The Romance of

Dolls
&
Teddy Bears

Ho Phi Le

Additional copies available at $39.95 each plus $6.25 postage from
Hobby House Press, Inc.
900 Frederick Street
Cumberland, MD 21502
or from your favorite bookstore or dealer

ISBN:0-87588-390-7

Table of Contents

I dedicate this book to:

Michele Durkson Clise

Carolyn Cook

Paul Hardin

Preface ...

I was born in Vietnam, a country where the past is very much a part of its people. In search of those wonder years, I found that my childhood days were memorable and very special. I remembered the little red train that I received from my beloved teacher one Christmas long ago. How fascinated I was with that generous gift. I would never forget those long recesses that my friends and I spent on the green grass playing with our imaginative toys. Oh, those tender years had so much innocence in the heart.

Now as I walk through the windy path of life, I learn to see the beauty in simple objects and treasure each day's memory in a special corner of my heart.

With the magic of a camera, I hope that I have captured the precious world of childhood dreams to share with you, my dear friends.

For this moment in time, let's leave our worried thoughts behind and take a magical journey along a memory lane that touches our souls and leads us to the romance of dolls, teddy bears and toys of long ago.

Unforgettable

A moment of waiting for the dawn of a new day to appear
is a moment for a dreamer to dream a
dream of things past.
Far away from the mountain high, the morning dew
rests peacefully on the green leaves till the first
sunlight touches the soft earth. In the wake of
the morning sun, faces of innocence appear
on your window of reverie.
Unforgettable is the only word that can
describe the feeling within your heart.

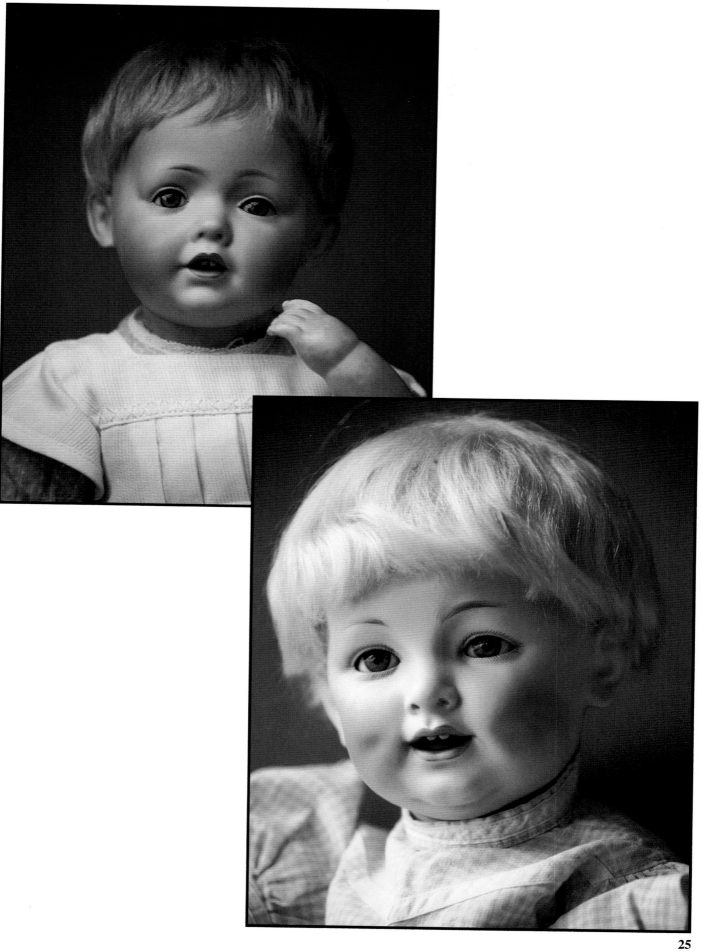

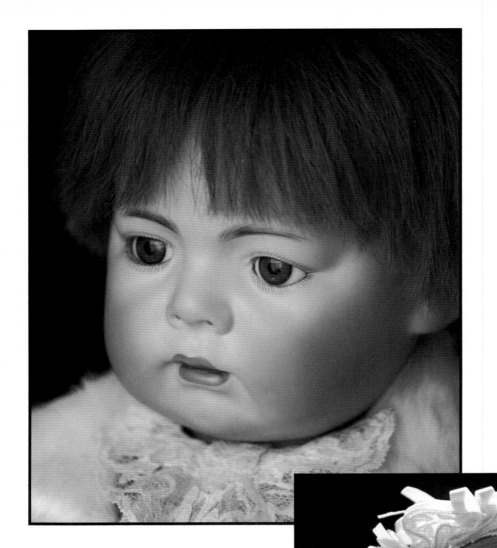

Schnuffy

Ms. Ophelia

Autumn's Secret

Whisper to me
The secret of autumn
Then I'll let my soul sing
To the falling leaves
In the cold gentle wind.

Whisper to me
Those happy memories
That I have lost
Long, long time ago.

Do you like
gathering memories
among the autumn leaves?

Winter Dreams

Imagine the first time you saw the white snow softly falling down from the grayish sky. Remember the icy feeling on your face as the snowflakes gently landed on your hair and shoulder. Your mind was at peace as you smiled at the evergreen trees shivering in the cold breeze. Snowflakes drifting softly down, one by one, as the earth is covered with the blanket of purity.

It is time to let your mind run free with the thoughts of yesteryears where all of your toys suddenly came to life. Enter now into the winter wonderland where all your dreams can come true.

Together always.

A Gentle Breeze of Spring

Through long winter days one's heart
dreams of sunny hours on the tapestry of green.
Suddenly the gentle breeze of spring
appears outside the window of dreams.
Bringing in flowers, of rainbow colors,
in the early morning light.
Making memories last on petals of roses
and forever holding the beauty of nature
in the spring time of gentle breezes.

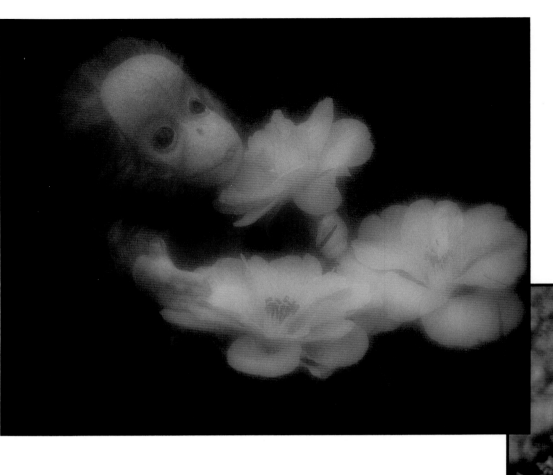

A
Summer
Day

Ah! Bear Hugs!

Do you hear
 the heartbeat of the ocean on a summer morn?
Do you feel
 the wind caressing your lovely face?
Do you smell
 the perfume of a new red rose?

Do you see
 the beauty in simple objects?
Do you remember
 your childhood dreams of years long past?
Here are the memories...
So come on in and hold on to these thoughts

On a lazy summer day.

133

143

Look at this, Teddy.

A day in the sun.

Oh, my! What a pretty
Steiff girl with her pretty
Steiff piggy.

Doing some "wishful thinking."

**Is this just a summer romance
or will we be together forever?**

Tender Moments

Oh, how we wish we could go back in time
to live again the memories of days gone by,
the time of carefree youth with so much
innocence in the heart.

But the past is forever behind us.
Let's leave those tender moments along
and embrace the happiness of our children
through their curious eyes
in the world of imagination.

Tenderly.

So Happy Together.

Oh, Little Boys.

Just Smile.

Love You Forever.

A Gentle Touch.

So Cute.

Tender Love.

Sing For Me, Little Bird.

Butterfly Free.

I Always Love You.

Just Me and You, Teddy.

On Sunny Hours.

Thinking of You.

Hold Me, Love.

Welcome, Dear Friend.

Oh, Teddy...

As the evening falls ....

In the wake of the late afternoon sun, time passes slowly through the lonely windswept hills. There are so many childhood memories that try to hold on to each other like a stream of thoughts lingering on one's mind on the sleepless night. Suddenly nothing is left but the shadow of the evening sky. Loneliness has come once again.

Acknowledgements

I'm very grateful to all of my friends who have shared with me not only their love for dolls and teddies but also a part of themselves in each photograph that I took. For that I thank you ...

Gary and Mary Ruddell for giving me a chance to express my artistic vision in my own special way.

Carolyn Cook for her expertise in creating this beautiful book and especially for her encouragement and friendship.

David Miller for his input on the cover.

Miko Smith for her talent and wonderful designs.

Michele Durkson Clise for teaching me to see the beauty in simple things.

Paul Hardin for being my best friend.

Hazel Coons for her love of dolls and for being my best doll friend.

Leone McMullen for her enthusiasm in collecting dolls and for all those wonderful tea parties.

Betty Lunz for her zest of life and for being so adorable.

Teresa Lehmbeck who sees things in a quiet way.

Julie Scott for sharing her collection and her beautiful daughter, Susan, with me.

Yvonne Baird for her knowledge in dolls and for having a great husband.

Bonnie Adie for being my gentle soul friend.

D.A. Horton who is my best bear friend.

Margaret Redpath who loves those E.J. faces as much as I do.

Rosalie Whyel for her generosity in sharing her fabulous collection with others.

Dolores Baker for understanding me so completely.

Carolyn Stone who finds well-loved objects so dear to her heart.

Connie Funk for being a perfect mother to Evan.

Alice Maffia for sharing her best dolls with me.

Tess Jones for sharing her terrific son, William, with me.

Annette Palm whose collection is one of the best in Washington.

Rosemary and Paul Volpp for sharing "Happy Anniversary" with the world.

Dottie Ayers for giving me the most memorable week in Maryland.

Barbara Baldwin for her friendship and for having two precious children.

Barbara Lauver who is my favorite teddy bear dealer.

Polly & Penny Zaneski for their passions in searching for objects of the past that touch the heart.

Nancy Sandberg for sharing her beautiful bears and for loving me like a son.

Khanh, Diep, Nga, Yen and Phuong, my five special sisters, whom I love dearly.

But most of all I want to thank you my dear mother whose love for me is higher than the highest mountain and deeper than the deepest ocean. I truly love you, Mom.

Captions

7. 25½in (65cm) portrait fashion Jumeau with a wooden body holding a 10in (25cm) closed-mouth Kestner pouty. *Bonnie Adie Collection.*

8. 20in (51cm) Steiff metal rod bear, circa 1903. *Barbara Lauver Collection.*

9. 24in (61cm) brown-tipped beige Steiff, circa 1926. "Happy Anniversary" was a wedding anniversary present from Paul Volpp to his wife Rosemary.

10. 16in (41cm) Kestner 220 toddler. *Private Collection.*

11. 21in (53cm) J.D.K. 245 *Hilda* character baby. *Private Collection.*

12. Top: 18in (46cm) all-original Jumeau fashion lady doll. *Yvonne Baird Collection.* Bottom: 23in (58cm) early Jumeau "9 E.J." Bébé. *Yvonne Baird Collection.*

13. 25in (64cm) E.J. marked "11" and has blue paperweight eyes and a closed mouth. *Collection of Margaret Redpath.*

14. 23in (58cm) early almond-eyed portrait Jumeau. *Yvonne Baird Collection.*

15. 23in (58cm) A.T. Bébé. *Rosalie Whyel Museum of Doll Art.*

16. A mystery child doll possibly made by Hertwig & Company of Katzhutte, Thuringia. *Rosalie Whyel Museum of Doll Art.*

17. 24in (61cm) incised H. Bébé. *Rosalie Whyel Museum of Doll Art.*

18. 21in (53cm) marked F.G. in block letters. *Yvonne Baird Collection.*

19. Top: 10in (25cm) early F.G. Bébé. *Yvonne Baird Collection.* Bottom: 25in (64cm) F.G. fashion lady doll. *Yvonne Baird Collection.*

20. Top: 20in (51cm) Bru Jne Bébé. *Bonnie Adie Collection.* Bottom: 22in (56cm) incised "10" on head, stamped Simonne body. *Rosalie Whyel Museum of Doll Art.*

21. 20in (51cm) white Steiff, circa 1905, and 21in (53cm) golden Steiff, circa 1909. *Private Collection.*

22. 25in (64cm) portrait Jumeau fashion. *Yvonne Baird Collection.*

23. Top: 20in (51cm) golden Steiff, circa 1907. *Private Collection.* Bottom: 19in (48cm) early Kestner, incised "13." *Private Collection.*

24. 33in (84cm) Long-face Triste Jumeau. *Yvonne Baird Collection.*

25. Top: 18in (46cm) J.D. Kestner 237 *Hilda* character baby. *Yvonne Baird Collection.* Bottom: 19in (48cm) Kestner 220 toddler. *Rosalie Whyel Museum of Doll Art.*

26. Top: 16in (41cm) Gebruder Heubach pouty. *Yvonne Baird Collection.* Bottom: 22in (56cm) portrait Jumeau fashion. *Yvonne Baird Collection.*

27. 27in (69cm) Circle Dot Bru. *Bonnie Adie Collection.*

28. Top: 33in (84cm) F.G. Bébé. *Bonnie Adie Collection.* Bottom: 34in (86cm) "C" Series Steiner. *Rosalie Whyel Museum of Doll Art.*

29. 23in (58cm) Open-mouth A.T. Bébé. *Rosalie Whyel Museum of Doll Art.*

30. 18in (46cm) marked 125 on head, possibly a Catterfelder Puppenfabrik character. *Rosalie Whyel Museum of Doll Art.*

31. 24in (61cm) Kestner 241. *Rosalie Whyel Museum of Doll Art.*

32. A large statue by F.B. & Company. *Julie Scott Collection.*

33. 15in (38cm) Bru fashion lady doll. *Julie Scott Collection.*

34. Top: 28in (71cm) Kämmer & Reinhardt 115A toddler. *Private Collection.* Bottom: 19in (48cm) Bru Jne. *Annette Palm Collection.*

35. 28in (71cm) Simon & Halbig 1488 toddler. *Private Collection.*

36. 25½in (65cm) fashion Jumeau with a wooden body. *Bonnie Adie Collection.*

37. Top: 26in (66cm) Circle Dot Bru. *Private Collection.* Bottom: 13in (33cm) Bru Bébé Teteur. *Bonnie Adie Collection.*

38. Top: 27in (69cm) Bru Jne. *Annette Palm Collection.* Bottom: 15in (38cm) all original Kämmer & Reinhardt 115A toddler. *Rosalie Whyel Museum of Doll Art.*

39. 25in (64cm) Figure "C" Series Steiner with bisque hands holding an 11in (28cm) Figure "A" Series Steiner. *Private Collection.*

40 and 41. *Michele Durkson Clise Collection.*

42 and 43. 28in (71cm) Kämmer & Reinhardt 115A toddler. *Private Collection.*

44. Top: 14in (36cm) Schuco yes/no bear, circa 1920s. *Private Collection.* Bottom: 24in (61cm) Steiff, circa 1920s. *Private Collection.*

45. Two 28in (71cm) Chad Valley bears, circa 1920s. *Private Collection.*

46. 22in (56cm) head incised "10X," early marked Jumeau body, holding a 14in (36cm) white Steiff, circa 1905. *Private Collection.*

47. 22in (56cm) Kämmer & Reinhardt 114 holding a 10in (25cm) gold Steiff, circa 1907. *Private Collection.*

48 and 49. 24in (61cm) Steiff, circa 1920s, 20in (51cm) white Steiff, circa 1909, 20 golden Steiff, circa 1905, and 10in (25cm) Schuco yes/no cat. *Private Collection.*

49. 20in (51cm) white Steiff, circa 1909. *Private Collection.*

50. 29in (74cm) F.G. lady fashion doll. *Betty Lunz Collection.*

51. 18in (46cm) all original Circle Dot Bru and 12in (31cm) Bru type. *Tess Jones Collection.*

52. 28in (71cm) Martha Chase doll named "Dolores." *Private Collection.*

53. 20in (51cm) Kämmer & Reinhardt 121 baby. *Private Collection.*

54. 24in (61cm) Steiff, circa 1920s, holding a 19in (48cm) E.8.J. Bébé. *Private Collection.*

55. Top: 14in (36cm) white Steiff dog, circa 1920s. *Private Collection.* Bottom: 17in (43cm) BSW (Bruno Schmidt of Walterhausen) 2972 named "Paul Jr." with 4in (10cm) Steiff *Hexi. Private Collection.*

56. 19in (48cm) Kämmer & Reinhardt 116A toddler. *Private Collection.*

57. 17in (43cm) J.D. Kestner 239 toddler. *Private Collection.*

58. A beautiful German deer, circa 1950s. *Private Collection.*

60. 28in (71cm) Kämmer & Reinhardt 117. *Private Collection.*

61. Top: 4in (10cm) golden Steiff, circa 1905. *Private Collection.* Bottom: 16in (41cm) brown-tipped German bear, circa 1920s. *Private Collection.*

62. 20in (51cm) Jumeau mechanical. *Annette Palm Collection.*

63. 20in (51cm) Steiff, circa 1905, and an antique tricycle. *Carolyn Stone Collection.*

64. Top: 14in (36cm) Hertel, Schwab & Company 125 toddler. *Private Collection.* Bottom: Two 17in (43cm) Käthe Kruse I Dolls. *Tess Jones Collection.*

65. 20in (51cm) center seam Steiff, circa 1907. *Leone McMullen Collection.*

66. 14in (36cm) Hertel, Schwab & Company 165 toddler and 9in (23cm) S.F.B.J. 245 with a five piece body. *Julie Scott Collection.*

67. Top: 19in (48cm) Käthe Kruse "Du Mein" and two 4in (10cm) leather dolls from France. *Tess Jones Collection.* Bottom: Two 21in (53cm) Käthe Kruse VIII Dolls. *Leone McMullen Collection.*

68. Top: 17in (43cm) A.T.-type Kestner, 15in (38cm) F.G. (Gaultier) with bisque arms and 10in (25cm) Jumeau "E.1.J." Bébé. *Julie Scott Collection.* Bottom: 17in (43cm) Tête Jumeau and 17in (43cm) A.T.-type Kestner. *Julie Scott Collection.*

69. 20in (51cm) white Steiff, circa 1920s. *Private Collection.*

71. 20in (51cm) Schuco yes/no bear, circa 1950s and 10in (25cm) replica of Steiff *Jackie* Bear. *Private Collection.*

72. 4in (10cm) Steiff, circa 1905, named "Lucky." *Private Collection.*

73. 21in (53cm) portrait Jumeau fashion doll. *Julie Scott Collection.*

74. 17in (43cm) Tête Jumeau. *Julie Scott Collection.*

75. 10in (25cm) Bru Brevete Bébé. *Julie Scott Collection.*

76. 26in (66cm) light gold Steiff, circa 1920s. *Polly and Penny Zaneski Collection.*

77. Two 10in (25cm) American bears, circa 1910 to 1920. *Polly and Penny Zaneski Collection.*

78. Top: Steiff Dog on wheels, circa 1910 to 1920, 30in (76cm) Tête Jumeau and a 10in (25cm) brown Steiff bear, circa 1907. *Polly and Penny Zaneski Collection.* Bottom: A wonderful group of early American teddy bears, circa 1905 to 1920s. *Polly and Penny Zaneski Collection.*

79. 26in (66cm) Jullien 9, 16in (41cm) white Steiff bear, circa 1905, and 28in (71cm) Jumeau with check mark. *Polly and Penny Zaneski Collection.*

80. 20in (51cm) white Steiff, circa 1909, 22in (56cm) Kley & Hahn baby, incised 13, and 3in (8cm) Schuco rabbit, circa 1950s. *Private Collection.*

81. Top: 10in (25cm) German dog, circa 1950s. *Private Collection.* Bottom: 20in (51cm) Steiff, circa 1905. *Private Collection.*

82. 21in (53cm) rare white Schuco yes/no musical bear, circa 1950s. *Private Collection.*

83. 20in (51cm) Schuco yes/no musical bear, circa 1950s. *Private Collection.*

84 and 85. 26in (66cm) light gold Steiff, circa 1920s. *Private Collection.*

85. Bottom: 17in (43cm) Schuco yes/no musical bear, circa 1950s, and two Steiff squirrels circa 1950s. *Private Collection.*

86. 12in (31cm) white Steiff, circa 1905, and a 6in (15cm) Steiff horse, circa 1960s. *Private Collection.*

88. 13in (33cm) Simon & Halbig 1279. *Julie Scott Collection.*

89. 16in (41cm) early R.D. (Rabery & Delphieu) Bébé. *Julie Scott Collection.*

90. 16in (41cm) J.D. Kestner toddler and 20in (51cm) Kestner 247 toddler with their 4in (10cm) Steiff cat, circa 1950s. *Annette Palm Collection.*

91. Top: 20in (51cm) light gold Steiff, circa 1930s. *Nancy Sandberg Collection.* Bottom: Two 18in (46cm) Steiff bears, circa 1907. *Barbara Baldwin Collection.*

92. Top: 24in (61cm) soft golden Steiff, circa 1920s and two *Bonzo* dogs by Chad Valley, circa 1920s. *Dottie Ayers Collection.* Bottom: 16in (41cm) chocolate-colored Steiff, circa 1905, and his Steiff bunny, circa 1950s. *Barbara Baldwin Collection.*

93. 24in (61cm) incised "Lori" by Swaine & Co. *Annette Palm Collection.*

94. 10in (25cm) Schuco yes/no orangutan, circa 1950s. *Private Collection.*

94 and 95. 20in (51cm) white center seam Steiff, circa 1905 with a group of friends. *Private Collection.*

96. 25in (64cm) open-mouth Tête Jumeau in an all original costume. *Private Collection.*

97. 14in (36cm) E.D. Bébé. *Teresa Lehmbeck Collection.*

98. 20in (51cm) Twyford bear, circa 1930s and 22in (56cm) Ernst Heubach 342. *Private Collection.*

99. Top: 10in (25cm) Steiff, circa 1907. *Dottie Ayers Collection.* Bottom: 18in (46cm) Kämmer & Reinhardt 101. *Leone McMullen Collection.*

100. Top: 21in (53cm) bisque figurines of German origin. *Julie Scott Collection.* Bottom: 16in (41cm) all original, unmarked fashion poupèe. *Teresa Lehmbeck Collection.*

101. 21in (53cm) Kämmer & Reinhardt 114. *Yvonne Baird Collection.*

102 10in (25cm) Steiff, circa 1907. *Dottie Ayers Collection.*

103. 18in (46cm) Kämmer & Reinhardt 116 toddler holding a tiny Cindy Martin bear. *Private Collection.*

104. 24in (61cm) Armand Marseille 353/8K. *Betty Lunz Collection.*

105. Top: 22in (56cm) Ernst Heubach 342. *Private Collection.* Bottom: 14in (36cm) Kestner 243. *Julie Scott Collection.*

106. Top: 14in (36cm) Heubach 10532 toddler and 16in (41cm) Kämmer & Reinhardt 114. *Leone McMullen Collection.* Bottom: Two 16in (41cm) Steiff bears, circa 1907-1910. *Dottie Ayers Collection.*

107. 24in (61cm) white center seam Steiff, circa 1905, listening to a beautiful antique wooden angel. *Dottie Ayers Collection.*

108. 17in (43cm) Hertel, Schwab & Co. 165 toddler. *Leone McMullen Collection.*

109. Top: 10in (25cm) *Paris Bébé* by Danel & Cie. Julie Scott Collection. Bottom: A well-loved 10in (25cm) teddy of unknown origin. *Dottie Ayers Collection.*

110. Top: 12in (31cm) Kämmer & Reinhardt 114. *Julie Scott Collection.* Bottom: 11in (28cm) Figure "A" Series Steiner and 10in (25cm) Jumeau "E.1.J." Bébé. *Julie Scott Collection.*

111. 13in (33cm) J.D. Kestner 245 black *Hilda* baby, 13in (33cm) J.D. Kestner 243 Oriental baby and 18in (46cm) Kämmer & Reinhardt 101. *Leone McMullen Collection.*

112. 20in (51cm) Twyford bear, circa 1930s and 4in (10cm) Steiff white mouse, circa 1950s. *Private Collection.*

113. Top: Two 20in (51cm) golden Steiff bears, circa 1907 holding a 4in (10cm) Steiff, circa 1950s. *Private Collection.* Bottom: 15in (38cm) Kämmer & Reinhardt 101 and 10in (25cm) white Steiff, circa 1905. *McMullen Collection.*

114. Top: 10in (25cm) Steiff, circa 1907. *Dottie Ayers Collection.* Bottom: 28in (71cm) light gold Steiff, circa 1915. *Private Collection.*

115. 21in (53cm) K*R 114 character girl. *Private Collection.*

116. 25in (64cm) all original Tête Jumeau. *Private Collection.*

117. Top: 12in (31cm) Bru-type Kestner. *Private Collection.* Bottom: Two 13in (33cm) Helvetic musical bears, circa 1920s. *Private Collection.*

118. 21in (53cm) rare, white Schuco yes/no musical bear, circa 1950s. *Private Collection.*

119. 24in (61cm) "C" Series Steiner. *Bonnie Adie Collection.*

121. 20in (51cm) Helvetic musical bear, circa 1920s, and 12in (31cm) creamy white Steiff, circa 1905. *Sandberg Collection.*

122. 26in (66cm) Kestner 249 and 10in (25cm) *Bonnie Babe.* *Private Collection.*

123. Top: 30in (76cm) open-mouth Jumeau. *Private Collection.* Bottom: 20in (51cm) Steiff, circa 1907 and his Steiff spider, circa 1950s. *Private Collection.*

124. Top: 16in (41cm) white Steiff, circa 1905. *Julie Scott Collection.* Bottom: 16in (41cm) *Uncle Sam. Julie Scott Collection.*

125. 20in (51cm) Martha Chase child doll with molded bobbed hair with her 18in (46cm) baby brother. *Yvonne Baird Collection.*

126. 16in (41cm) "C" Series Steiner and 20in (51cm) kicking Steiner. *Private Collection.*

127. 17in (43cm) Gebruder Heubach 5636 and 17in (43cm) Kämmer & Reinhardt 114. *Annette Palm Collection.*

128. 22in (56cm) Kämmer & Reinhardt 115A toddler and 5in (13cm) teddy created by Becky Burke.

129. 11in (28cm) early Kestner pouty, incised "5." *Private Collection.*

130. Top: 18in (46cm) Schoenhut. *Private Collection.* Bottom: A group of Schoenhut dolls from 16in (41cm) to 20in (51cm). *Private Collection.*

131. 10in (25cm) "A" Series Steiner and 14in (36cm) "C" Series Steiner. *Private Collection.*

132. 12in (31cm) Steiff bear, circa 1907, a large unmarked wax doll, and 12in (31cm) Ideal teddy, circa 1910 to 1920. *Yvonne Baird Collection.*

133. Top: 14in (36cm) Kestner 226 baby, 13in (33cm) Armand Marseille 248, and 19in (48cm) Kamkins. *Tess Jones Collection.* Bottom: 27in (69cm) Kämmer & Reinhardt 115A toddler and 9in (23cm) Motchmann-type baby. *Tess Jones Collection.*

134. 28in (71cm) early F.G. Bébé. *Private Collection.*

135. 24in (61cm) Tête Jumeau. *Julie Scott Collection.*

136. 18in (46cm) Catterfelder Puppenfabrik 220 character child. *Leone McMullen Collection.*

137. Two 21in (53cm) Käthe Kruse VIII dolls and 16in (41cm) American teddy, circa 1910. *Private Collection.* Inset: Two Steiff dolls with their Steiff pig and duck on wheels, circa 1910. *Barbara Lauver Collection.*

138. 21in (53cm) Martha Chase baby. *Tess Jones Collection.*

139. Top: Two early cloth dolls of unknown origin. *Yvonne Baird Collection.* Bottom: 24in (61cm) black Martha Chase doll. *Yvonne Baird Collection.*

140. Top: Two 14in (36cm) Martha Chase dolls. *Polly and Penny Zaneski Collection.* Bottom: A wonderful group of Steiff bears and animals, circa 1905-1960. *Barbara Baldwin Collection.*

141. Two 20in (51cm) American bears, circa 1907. *Polly and Penny Zaneski Collection.*

142. 17in (43cm) Gebruder Heubach 734/12X and 12in (31cm) Q.J. baby. *Annette Palm Collection.*

143. Top: 170. 12in (31cm) white Steiff, circa 1905. *Nancy Sandberg Collection.* Bottom: 28in (71cm) Kämmer & Reinhardt 117, 28in (71cm) Simon & Halbig 1488 toddler, and 12in (31cm) Steiff bear. *Annette Palm Collection.*

144 and 145. 20in (51cm) white center seam Steiff, circa 1905 and 21in (53cm) golden Steiff, circa 1909. *Private Collection.*

145. 20in (51cm) Steiff, circa 1907. *Private Collection.*

146. Top: 18in (46cm) Käthe Kruse and 16in (41cm) Steiff, circa 1904. *Annette Palm Collection.* Bottom: 24in (61cm) unmarked black composition doll and 18in (46cm) Ideal bear, circa 1905. *Annette Palm Collection.*

147. 29in (74cm) DEP and 15in (38cm) Kämmer & Reinhardt 115A toddler. *Annette Palm Collection.*

148. 24in (61cm) Kämmer & Reinhardt 116A toddler and 12in (31cm) Steiff, circa 1907. *Annette Palm Collection.*

149. 31in (79cm) S.F.B.J. 236 doll and 18in (46cm) Ideal bear, circa 1905. *Annette Palm Collection.*

150. 24in (61cm) Martha Chase doll and 20in (51cm) white center seam Steiff, circa 1905. *Carolyn Stone Collection.*

151. 11in (28cm) P.M. (Otto Reinecke) 950 and 19in (48cm) Gebruder Heubach 5689. *Annette Palm Collection.*

152. Top: 18in (46cm) Roosevelt bears, circa 1910s. *Zaneski Collection.* Bottom: Steiff doll, circa 1910, with Steiff pig. *Lauver Collection.*

153. 20in (51cm) American bear, circa 1910, with very rare Steiff fish. *Sandberg Collection.*

154. 24in (61cm) gold mohair Steiff; circa 1905. *Sandberg Collection.*

155. Top: 20in (51cm) Steiff bears, circa 1907. *Sandberg Collection.* Bottom: 22in (56cm) English teddy with gold mohair, circa 1920s. *Sandberg Collection.*

157. 22in (56cm) *Baby Ruki* created by Annette Himstedt and two 16in (41cm) teddies created by Jeanette Warner. *Private Collection.*

158 and 159. William Jones and his 20in (51cm) Steiff doll, circa 1910. *Private Collection.*

159. William Jones playing with his 20in (51cm) Steiff bear, circa 1905. *Private Collection.*

160. Top: Emi and her wonderful Steiff teddy, circa 1905. *Private Collection.* Bottom: 13in (33cm) J.D. Kestner named *Baby Jean* and 20in (51cm) teddy created by Jeanette Warner. *Private Collection.*

161. Susan Scott and her 21in (53cm) F.G. Bébé. *Julie Scott Collection.*

162. Bret holding a 10in (25cm) Steiff bear and Lindsay reading to a 15in (38cm) Kestner 211. *Private Collection.*

163. Top: Lindsay Decker and her little Kestner 211. Bottom: 16in (41cm) Steiff Jackie Bear, circa 1950s. *Dottie Ayers Collection.*

164. 27in (69cm) Kley & Hahn 169 toddler and his little Steiff bird, circa 1950s. *Private Collection.*

165. 20in (51cm) and 12in (31cm) Steiff bears circa 1907. *Nancy Sandberg Collection.*

166. Connie and Evan and 12in (31cm) Steiff, circa 1905.

167. Jessica Baldwin with her 18in (46cm) Ideal bear, circa 1903. *Barbara Baldwin Collection.*

168. 28in (71cm) Simon & Halbig 1488 toddler and his Steiff dog, circa 1948. *Private Collection.*

169. Top: 17in (43cm) S.F.B.J. 252 and 12in (31cm) Steiff bear circa 1907. *Annette Palm Collection.* Bottom: 24in (61cm) Steiff bear circa 1907 and a large Steiff deer circa 1940s. *Barbara Baldwin Collection.*

170. 16in (41cm) Hertel, Schwab & Co. 165 baby and 13in (33cm) Steiff bear, circa 1907. *Rosalie Whyel Museum of Doll Art.*

171. Julia Whyel with her little 13in (33cm) Steiff bear. *Private Collection.*